Yonge Street, *Toronto's main street, is busy rain or shine, sleet or snow. A safe and interesting place to take a walk, night or day.*

Toronto's history begins back in the 1700's when the French and Iroquoian nations established this location as an important port for trade, commerce and transportation. As a result of two great fires, an American invasion, and other turbulent occurrences, much of early

Toronto is no more, but unlike some cities of modern distinction, Toronto embraces its past by preserving its historical heritage. Take a leisurely drive anywhere in Toronto and you will surely come across some of the finest architecture that constantly reminds us

of earlier times. You can easily step into Toronto's humble beginnings with a visit to one of the many historical landmarks that are located within the city limits. **Old Fort York and Pioneer Village** are two living exhibits that recreate life as it was a hundred years ago. Here you can feel the drama of one of the fiercest battles in this city's peaceful history or taste the fresh bread that today is still baked in massive stone fireplaces.

Ontario Legislative Buildings, Queen's Park

Toronto's Old City Hall,
now being used as a courthouse

University College at the **University of Toronto**

Casa Loma

*The **Oak Room**, one of **Casa Loma's** beautifully decorated rooms*

Sir Henry Pellatt

Ask any Torontonian to name the most famous historical site within the city and they will be sure to answer **Casa Loma**. On the brow of a hill, overlooking Toronto, the striking silhouette of a massive castle stirs the imagination. Based on a life-long fascination with European Castles, Sir Henry Pellatt a stock market millionaire, borrowed the most pleasing elements of Norman, Gothic and Romanesque styles to create Casa Loma in 1914 at a cost of $3 million dollars. Both formal and informal gardens adorn the beautifully landscaped grounds beckoning visitors on a leisurely stroll through this splendid six-acre estate. At every turn your senses are delighted by dancing fountains, unusual sculptures, and the dazzling, everchanging colours of a Canadian garden.

The **Royal York Hotel,** *one of the oldest hotels in the city*

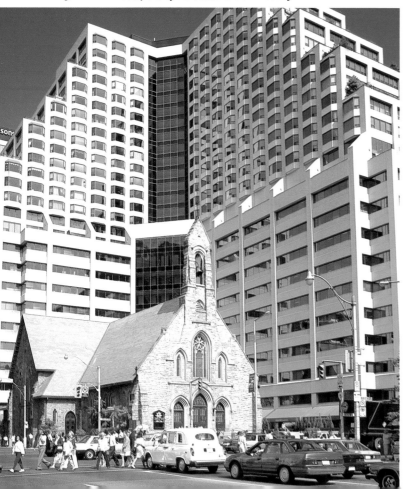

A house in the **Beaches**

What makes Toronto a visual experience unrivaled by any other city in the world is the way that it combines old world charm with its new cosmopolitan character. This breathtaking city serves as an unparalleled exhibit to mankinds architectural brilliance.

Corner of **Bloor St.** *and* **Avenue Road** *-
the old and the new*

*A view along **Front Street** showing the old **Flat Iron Building** and the new **B.C.E. Place** behind it.*

Old City Hall

*The architectural design of Toronto's **City Hall**, with its two semi-circular buildings, portrays dignity and daring.*

When Finnish architect Viljo Revell won the international competition for the design of **Toronto's New City Hall** in 1957, the city began its transformation from a conservative community to a world trend-setting centre. Even today City Hall stands out as one of the most recognizable landmarks in the world. The real focal point, however, is the plaza in front of City Hall, **Nathan Phillips Square** — named after the mayor who made it happen — which supplies what every city needs but few possess: a meeting place for the whole community. The Square is used by some to have lunch on a sunny day by the fountain and pond, which turns into a popular skating rink in the winter. It is also a venue for concerts, art exhibits and political demonstrations.

*Taking a break in **Nathan Phillips Square***

*The **Royal Bank Tower**, with windows glazed with gold, shimmers magnificently day and night.*

Since the construction of City Hall, Toronto has become the grounds for some of the most impressive buildings found anywhere. Massive steel and glass skyscrapers dominate Toronto's downtown areas such as **University Avenue, Bloor Street**, and world renowned **Bay Street**, which is home to the second largest **Stock Exchange** in North America. Every day, Toronto continues to grow with new and more fascinating buildings springing up everywhere.

Toronto's financial district featuring the **Royal Bank** *building,* **Commerce Court** *and the* **Toronto Dominion Centre**

Canada Geese pay a call at the CN Tower and SkyDome.

The Toronto Island Ferry and the CN Tower

Without a doubt one of the most spectacular landmarks in the world has to be Toronto's **CN Tower**. It has been said that every visitor should start any sight-seeing expedition here. The reason is simple. In addition to being a breathtaking sight in itself, the tower offers a dazzling 360 degree view of the city that you just won't find anywhere else. Opened in 1976, the CN Tower is much more than just a huge monument; it is a communications tower, a revolving restaurant, a nightclub, a long elevator ride and the world's tallest freestanding structure at 1815 feet, making it almost twice as tall as the Eiffel Tower. The top of the Tower was lowered into place by a helicopter in 1975. On a clear day, you can see the spray of Niagara Falls from the Tower's observation deck.

*The **CN Tower** never fails
to impress from any angle.*

*Opening Day at **SkyDome**.*

*Toronto's **SkyDome**, amazing both night and day*

One of the more recent additions to Toronto's already captivating skyline is the **SkyDome**. This magnificent structure remains one of the most talked about venues in the city. But "The Dome" is much more than just a civic landmark; it is the first major sports stadium to be topped by a fully retractable roof. On the site is a 348-suite hotel, a 650-seat restaurant, and an array of fast good options,

three bars, meeting facilities, a health and fitness club and **SkyPlace**, a combination of retail outlets, offices and an information centre. Though SkyDome has become a major Toronto concert venue, the complex's most important function is as home to both the **Toronto Blue Jays**, baseball's 1992 and 1993 **World Series** Champions, and the **Toronto Argonauts** football team.

Aside from the day-to-day grind, Torontonians relish the fact that nestled in amongst our many skyscrapers are neighbourhoods that give our city its distinctive home-like feel. From the **Annex** to **Yorkville**, from the Toronto Islands to **High Park**, each and every section of Toronto resonates with its own special vibrato. As in many big cities Toronto has its cultural neighbourhoods like **Little Italy, Chinatown, and Little Athens**, and the vast majority of people who live in the city will trumpet the value of our ethnic districts and how they enhance the city. But, Toronto is not only divided into little ethnic pockets. Many of our neighbourhoods are unique for reasons defined more by attitude than by culture. Take, for example, the laid back, Californian attitude of **The Beaches** in contrast to the carefully manicured gentility of **Forest Hill** or the old money aura of **Rosedale**. More than anything else it is the complexion of our urban neighbourhoods that give Toronto its diverse character.

*Sailing on **Lake Ontario***

Street signs mark the past as well as the present.

Cabbagetown takes its name from the early residents' habit of growing cabbages on the front lawn, this delightful neigbourhood has been transformed from a low-cost housing project to one of Toronto's more "upwardly mobile" areas.

◀ *Toronto by day along the shores of **Lake Ontario***

Immigrants hold forth at the Greenview Fruit Market.

*An afternoon on **Bloor Street***

*Toronto as seen from the **CN Tower***

Toronto's **Chinatown** rivals San Francisco's in size and excitement. The myriad of shops and restaurants, and the hustle and bustle of activity has added a wonderful dimension to Toronto's personality.

North York, one of the six cities and boroughs making up **Metropolitan Toronto**, grew tremendously in the 1980's, creating it's own "downtown" along north **Yonge Street**, with exciting architecture alongside more staid municipal buildings. Shown above is the **North York City Hall**.

Brunswick Avenue, a quiet downtown residential street

*Millions have come and gone through the **Prince's Gates** at the **C.N.E.**, or "**The Ex**" as the world's largest annual fair is popularly called. This August event features air shows, aqua shows, horse trials and concerts. The games and rides of the midway are among the most popular attractions.*

A big city needs to offer plenty of attractions and entertainment venues for its citizens and visitors alike, and Toronto provides some of the best. There is lots to do and see in the city, whether your taste is upscale shopping, or meandering through the open markets of **Kensington** and **Chinatown**, where the most recent immigrants offer produce and wares at prices to be determined in typical market fashion.

*Mirvish Village, a shopping area near **Honest Ed's** was developed by "Honest" Ed Mirvish, himself. It boasts several fine restaurants and upscale shops, only steps away from the phenomenal bargain house that made Ed Mirvish famous.*

Yorkville, once a little village of well-kept Victorian row-houses, became the centre of "flower power" in the 1960's, with head shops and coffee houses that saw the likes of Joni Mitchell and Gordon Lightfoot when they were just starting out as entertainers. Places like "The Riverboat" have now been replaced by discotheques, art shops, couturiers, interior decorators and restaurants for a more chic clientele.

Kensington Market It is reassuring to know that there are still some places where haggling over prices is still acceptable.

Toronto in the summertime is a pretty special place to be. **Paramount Canada's Wonderland** is an amusement park that covers 121 hectares and is filled with rides, displays, concerts, shows and a multitude of other diversions. Similar to Wonderland is the **Canadian National Exhibition**. For Torontonians, The **CNE** (or **EX** as it is more commonly called) is sentimental part of summer in the city. It is, in fact, the world's largest outdoor fair: and in addition to the classic midway rides, you will find various exhibits as well as enticing games of chance and skill. In short, the "Ex" offers the best of a good old country fair right in the heart of the city.

*The **Queen Elizabeth Building** at the CNE*

__Magic Mountain__ at Paramount Canada's Wonderland ▶

*The **CNE Midway** offers rides and candy floss among its many attractions.*

While the **Ex** is open only from mid-August to Labour Day in September, **Ontario Place** is open all summer long. This park-like entertainment complex is built over three man-made islands that jut out into Lake Ontario. Here you can enjoy a movie on the "**Cinespheres**" six-storey screen or explore a floating museum on a WWII Destroyer. Other attractions include a children's playground, an outdoor concert hall, a wide assortment of restaurants and pubs and plenty of open parkland.

Another summer place to visit, especially with children, is **Centreville**. This cosy amusement area on Centre Island may be no match for Canada's Wonderland or the EX when it comes to size, but when it comes to offering kids a great place to play, Centreville is ideal.

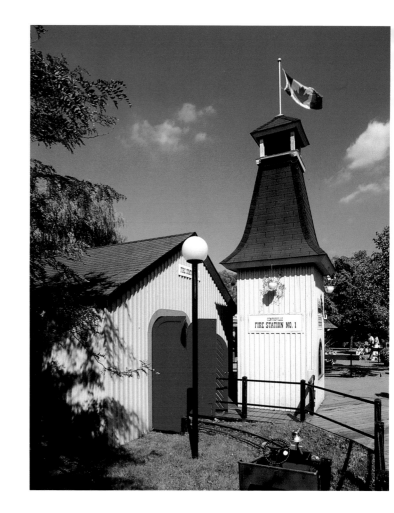

*An aerial view of **Ontario Place***

__Ontario Place__ water ride with the __HMCS Haida__ in background

*A pond in **High Park**, Toronto's largest park, located in the city centre.*

Queen's Quay Terminal, *part of the once mighty Reichman Empire, is a testament to good taste and design.*

Feeding black-footed penguins at the **Metro Toronto Zoo**. *Considered to be one of the world's best, Toronto's zoo exhibits more than 4,000 animals in settings that most closely resemble the animals' natural habitats.*

Black Creek Pioneer Village *is a great place to spend a day in the past.*

High Park has been called Toronto's answer to New York's Central Park and London's Hyde Park. The land for the park was donated to the city in 1873 by **John Howard**, a wealthy Torontonian and tea-totaller, who insisted on a provision that liquor would never be sold in the park. He would surely approve, however, of the beautiful nature trails, the wild ravines and the formal gardens which now enhance his old homestead.

Harbourfront, on the the other hand, is a place where you can enjoy an outdoor drink or listen to one of the many free, live musical performances, all overlooking Lake Ontario.

*There is no other way to describe **Edwards Gardens** other than to say that it is a wonderful place to seek refuge from the hectic pace of a thriving metropolis. Vast arrays of colourful blooms, featuring rockeries, rustic bridges, greenhouses and waterfalls highlight this beautiful park.*

Ontario Science Centre *in autumn*

*Visiting the **Ontario Science Centre** can be a hair-raising experience!*

When the cool northern breezes start lofting into the city, it becomes time to discover Toronto from indoors. The **Ontario Science Centre** is a cross between a museum and a pinball arcade. Most of the 700 elaborate exhibits depicting the advances of technology through the ages require audience participation. In a random stroll through the halls you might encounter an electrostatic generator that makes your hair stand on end, tape decks and TV cameras that you activate by pedalling furiously on a bicycle, a simulation of a moon landing, and 15 mini-theatres where you can sit down and watch brief film and slide presentations. Not only is the Science Centre a marvel of architectural and environmental harmony, it is also a really fun place to learn.

Air Canada Centre

With the success of the **Blue Jays** in recent years one might think that baseball was the only game in town. Not so! For decades now Torontonians have painfully watched the ups and downs of their most beloved sports team, **The Toronto Maple Leafs**. Watching this National Hockey League team play at the **Air Canada Centre** is a favourite winter pastime. Until February 1999, the Leafs played their home games at the beloved Maple Leaf Gardens, the 1920s steel shrine that remains a popular venue for concerts and events. Most will agree that Toronto is first and foremost a hockey town. Of course it's also a basketball town since the National Basketball Association's **Toronto Raptors** hit the court. Still, if you enjoy spectator games of another nature, Toronto offers a year-round smorgasbord of sports: Professional golf, tennis, football and soccer are also on the minds of Toronto sports fans.

Toronto Raptors

36

Historic **Maple Leaf Gardens**

Toronto Blue Jays at the *SkyDome*

*The talent at **Roy Thompson Hall** shines. Accoustics in this concert hall are impeccable.*

Ford Centre For The Performing Arts

Aside from its more famous concert venues such as **The O'Keefe Centre or Roy Thomson Hall**, Toronto boasts some of the finest theatre facilities found anywhere. The **Elgin & Winter Garden Theatres** are the only functioning double-decker theatres in the world and have played host to such prestigious troupes as the Royal Shakespeare Company and Dublin's Abbey Players. Almost 70 years after it originally opened its doors, the **Pantages Theatre** re-opened to reveal to Toronto audiences what meticulous craftsmanship and 18 million dollars can do.

*The refurbished **Pantages Theatre***

An evening at the **Royal Alexandra Theatre** is how an evening at the theatre is meant to be. The theatre's red plush seats and baroque ornamentation were saved from the wrecking ball in 1962 by discount department store tycoon Ed Mirvish. Mr. Mirvish restored the "**Royal Alex**" to its original grandeur and, using the same business acumen that made him a very wealthy retailer, turned the theatre into a profitable operation.

Thousands of visitors come to see the Egyptian Mummies

*Arms and armour, costumes and textiles can be found at the **ROM***

Royal Ontario Museum

Toronto's museums offer exhibits to suit every palate. You can discover everything from **Group of Seven** masterpieces to the National Hockey League's **Stanley Cup** on display in Toronto. Located in the heart of **Chinatown**, the **Art Gallery of Ontario** is undoubtedly one of the continent's truly impressive fine art museums. It contains twenty large galleries highlighting Western art, Renaissance art, Impressionist, Post-impressionist and Modernist works. A particularly impressive feature is the **Henry Moore Sculpture Centre**, that displays 893 works — the largest public collection in the world — by the renowned English sculptor. Another highlight of this museum is the Canadian wing, devoted to Canadian art from the past three centuries, including several works by members of the Group of Seven. Another "must see" is **The Royal Ontario Museum**. This awe-inspiring museum displays spectacular exhibits that include dinosaurs and life-like replicas of bats to the famous Far Eastern collection, which includes three 13th-century Chinese temple wall paintings and a monumental Ming tomb.

41

*Looking southwest at **The Royal Ontario Museum***

*Chinese temple art in the **Bishop White Gallery***

*A full-scale replica of the Montreal Canadiens' dressing room is one of the many popular exhibits ⟨...⟩ the **Hockey Hall of Fame**.*

Art Gallery of Ontario

*Dancers at **Caribana**, the largest Caribbean Festival in North America, held in Toronto each summer, demonstrate their wild and colourful costumes.*

As befits one of North America's fastest-growing cities, Toronto celebrates everything, from the arts to ethnic heritage, with well-organized flair. In late June, the **Metro International Caravan** transforms more than forty locations across the city into "pavilions" featuring the crafts, music, dance, food and drink of the many nationalities that have blended together to make Toronto what it is today. The ethnic flavour gets more specific in August with **Caribana**. Starting with a brilliant parade, this **Caribbean festival** takes over the Toronto islands for a weekend of steel bands, reggae and "jump-up." Fall brings the **International Film Festival**, fast winning a reputation as one of the best-organized, widest-ranging and friendliest film spectaculars anywhere.

Yonge Street, *Toronto's "main drag" featuring the landmark "Sam the Record Man".*

Once you have examined Toronto's landscape and enjoyed the city's cultural exhibits, you are ready to take in some of the best shopping found in North America. Whether you are in the mood for some serious bargain-hunting or a break-the-bank shopping spree, you're in the right place. From the boutique-lined streets of the lavish **Bloor/Yorkville** district to the bohemian collection of shops in the **Queen Street** fashion district, Metropolitan Toronto has stores to satisfy every taste, and every style. **The Eaton Centre** was hailed as an architectural marvel when it opened in 1977 and it remains a stunning example of how beautifully designed an enclosed shopping complex can be. The mall stretches along a portion of famous Yonge Street and includes over 330 shops and services. **Yorkville**, Toronto's most fashionable shopping district, boasts a list of tenants which reads like a "who's who" of international retailing.

Queen's Quay Terminal Building, once a warehouse on the waterfront was renovated in 1983 by Olympia and York. The multi-million dollar face-lift created an extraordinary shopping and condominium complex that housed some of Toronto's finest and most interesting stores. If you are one to "shop till you drop", you can resuscitate yourself in the lakeside restaurant that is part of the complex.

*Shopping at the **Queen's Quay Terminal Building***

With one million square feet of retail floor space and over 300 stores, the **Eaton Centre** has become one of the world's busiest shopping complexes and tourist attractions, located in the heart of the city.

For another kind of shopping, the **St. Lawrence Market** offers a farmers' market on Saturdays and an antiques and collectibles market on Sundays. Or, if you prefer bargains galore and the lowest prices in town, **Honest Ed's** will not disappoint you. Starting with his parent's corner store, and built piecemeal thereafter by incorporating neighbouring properties, Ed Mirvish became one of Toronto's great entrepreneurs. Using **Honest Ed's** as his economic base, he went on to build restaurants out of warehouses — **Ed's Warehouse** — and revitalized Toronto's **Royal Alexandra Theatre** and with it Toronto theatre as a whole.

Honest Ed's *Ed Mirvish's massive discount store "where only the floors are crooked" remains a Toronto landmark.*

Street vendors abound and are always ready to offer you a smile.

An enticing international dining adventure can be yours any and every night of the week because Toronto's more than 4,000 restaurants represent a virtual United Nations of dining options. Toronto's culinary world tour covers everything from California-inspired spa food to the robust fare of eastern Europe; from Japanese sushi to Scandinavian delicacies. No matter what your preference, there is a restaurant somewhere in town that's made to order.

*Fine restaurants which feature world renowned chefs are found throughout the city but for those with simpler tastes, a streetside **hot dog vendor** will be happy to take your order.*

Pearson Airport

*Once in the city, the **Toronto Transit Commissions's** subway system is a favourite, and convenient, means of transportation.*

For air travellers, getting into and out of the city is primarily achieved through **The Lester B. Pearson International Airport**. The airport is a virtual beehive of activity. It handles millions of travellers each year making it the third busiest airport in North America. Smaller Airports such as the **City Centre Airport** on Toronto Island, are used mainly for private aircraft and shorter distance commercial flights. If you prefer to travel by train, Toronto also incorporates a rail system that moves people in and out of the various provinces as well as from its outlying municipalities of **Scarborough** and **Mississauga**.

*Toronto is exceedingly proud of its new **Terminal 3** at **Lester B. Pearson International Airport**.*

City Centre Airport

*A streetcar on the **Queen Street** line*

Within the city you'll find living proof that the automobile is not the only answer to getting around. This is one North American city with an efficient, clean, safe public transit system which combines subways, streetcars and buses to take you from wherever you are to wherever you're going. Of course you can always opt to use one of the thousands of taxi cabs available at your disposal 24 hours a day, or hop a ride in one of Toronto's famous Rickshaw buggies.

*Many commuters and tourists opt for alternatives, like the **GO Transit**, to driving in busy Toronto traffic.*

*A Sunday escape on the **Island Ferry***

*Toronto as seen from the **Islands***

*Boaters relax at the **Island** docks*

By day or night **Toronto** has something to offer everyone. People from everywhere in a city with everything, all living together with the greatest of ease. There are towers of gold that thrust ever skyward. There are Victorian homes under a mantle of green. There are great stores and markets, museums and galleries, first-rate live theatre and exquisite cuisine. In Toronto, there is a whole world to see.

Toronto's **Harbourfront** at dusk ▶

Published and Distributed by
Irving Weisdorf & Co. Ltd.
2801 John Street,
Markham, Ontario L3R 2Y8

Text by
Michael Landesburg

Designed by
David Villavera

ISBN:0-921978-36-7

Photographer	Page
G. Abel	36
R. Arlt-Chanter	25b, 60h, 59a
G. Briand	22a, 23a, 43b, 53c, 58b, 60g, 61a
C.N.E.	28b
The Postcard Factory	3, 20/21, 37a, 38b, 46, 54b
G. Dillon	30a, 30b, 31b
H. Ehricht	9a, 9b
L. Fisher	Front cover, Back cover, 2, 4/5, 6, 7b, 8, 10a, 10b, 10c, 11a, 12a, 12b, 13, 14, 15b, 16, 17a, 17b, 17c, 19, 22b, 24b, 25a, 26b, 27a, 28a, 37b, 38a, 39a, 40, 41c, 47b, 49, 50b, 51a, 52b, 53a, 53b, 56, 57, 60c, 60e, 61b, 61d, 62/63
H. Georgi	26a
GO Transit Photo	58a
P. Halsall	48a, 48b
D. Haneda	33b
A. Hayt / NBA Photos	36b (All Rights Reserved)
G. Matthews	24a
G. Romany	11b, 15a, 31a, 43a, 51b, 54a, 55a, 59, 60d
B. Rondel	33a
F. Scott	32a, 34, 60a, 60f
P. Sellar	47a, 52a, 52c
I. Steer	18
B. Stoneham	60b
V. Tate	29, 44, 45
I. Weisdorf	3b, 7a, 23b, 32b, 42a, 50a, 61c, 61e